by

Big Chief I-SPY

Polystyle Publications Limited
382/386 Edgware Road
London W2 1EP

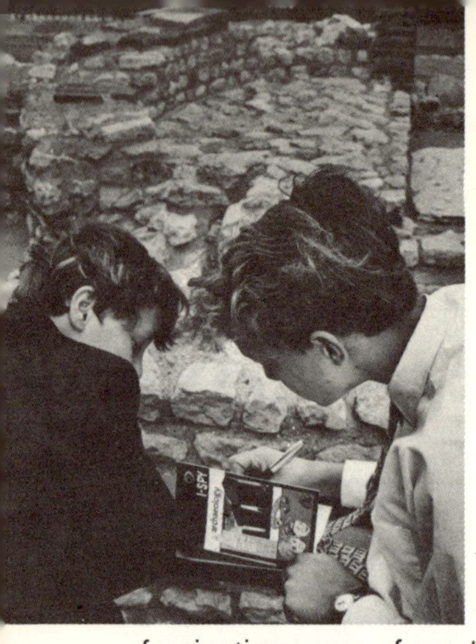

You might be digging in the garden when you come across a strange looking flint. Pick it up. The last person to touch it might have been Stone Age Man thousands of years ago. He might have used it to skin animals. Just think, you could be holding one of the earliest tools ever made.

I-SPY Archaeology tells you about Stone Age flints, Bronze Age weapons, Roman glass and more. It takes you through the fascinating years of pre-history from 550,000 BC to the end of the Roman occupation.

This is a difficult book to score for. Some things you'll see in museums, others at archaeological sites. Archaeologists work hard to protect our past and tell us more about it. Excavation is a highly skilled task so leave it to the experts. Just keep your eyes open. You'll find lots to keep you busy—and to score for in this book. Soon *you'll* be an expert.

When your scores total 1,250 points you may award yourself the rank of ARCHAEOLOGIST Second Class. When they reach a complete total of 1,500 points you are entitled to the rank of ARCHAEOLOGIST First Class; you may then send your book to me, and I shall return it to you stamped with my personal seal. Your certificate of rank is on the inside back cover of this book.

Here's your path through pre-history, from the days when man first learnt to use flint to the days, many thousands of years later, when he had learnt how to use glass.

As you work your way through I-SPY Archaeology refer back to this diagram: it will name each period for you, tell you how old it is and the kind of thing produced then.

BRONZE SPEARHEAD
LATER BRONZE AGE 1,000 BC

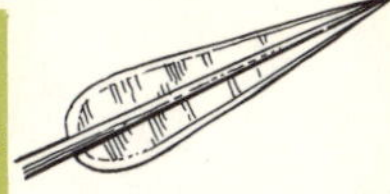

FLINT HAND AXE
PALAEOLITHIC 550,000 BC STONE AGE

POTTERY BOWL
IRON AGE A 450 BC

BARBED ANTLER SPEARHEAD
MESOLITHIC 12,000 BC STONE AGE

BROOCH
IRON AGE B 250 BC

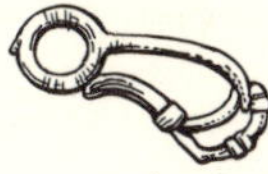

STONE AXE
NEOLITHIC 3,000 BC STONE AGE

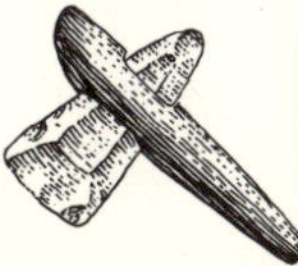

BRONZE HELMET
IRON AGE C 75 BC

FOOD VESSEL
EARLY BRONZE AGE 1,850 BC

ROMAN GLASS BOTTLE
ROMAN BRITAIN AD 43

Stone Age Though his tools and weapons are now in museums all over the country, actual remains of Stone Age Man himself are very rare. For instance, the famous human remains found at Swanscombe, Kent, are only fragments of a skull. From these, however, archaeologists can tell that Swanscombe Man lived 250,000 years ago, belonged to the Acheulian culture, and used tools like the hand-axe pictured here (*above*).

Gradually Stone Age Man learnt how to make better flint tools by using an anvil and indirect force. We call these flints Clactonian (*below*).

Score for seeing either the Acheulian hand-axe or the Clactonian flake tool.

Mine was a: ....

....

At: ....

......................*Museum* Score **70**

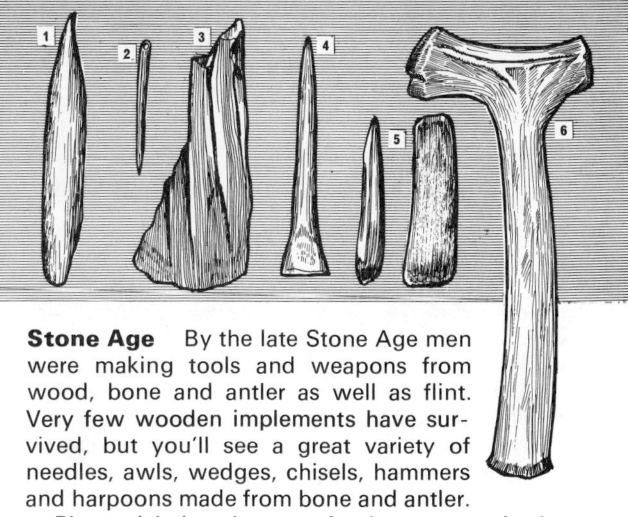

Stone Age By the late Stone Age men were making tools and weapons from wood, bone and antler as well as flint. Very few wooden implements have survived, but you'll see a great variety of needles, awls, wedges, chisels, hammers and harpoons made from bone and antler.

Pictured below is part of a harpoon and, above, (1) awl made of polished antler (2) polished bone needle (3) horse bone from which slivers have been gouged out for needles (4) bone awl (5) antler wedge or chisel—shown from two angles (6) antler hammer.

Mine was a: ....

At: ....

....

......*Museum* Score **30**

Stone/Early Bronze Age

Britain became separated from the continent during the Mesolithic period (about 12,000 BC to 3,000 BC). Stone weapons were now very sophisticated—the flint arrowhead below was made during the Early Bronze Age and is 'barbed' and 'tanged'. Small tools or weapons, known as microliths (*above*), seldom more than an inch long, were often flaked into geometric patterns.

The leister (*left*), a fish spear with barbed antler points, was used particularly for catching pike. The skeletons of fish 'that got away' have been found with broken leister points still in them.

Where did you see any of these three things?

....

.... Score **60**

FLINT ARROWHEAD

LEISTER OR FISH SPEAR

BARB

TANG

Stone/Early Bronze Age Hut Circle On the Devon and Yorkshire moors you'll see hut circles—the remains of Neolithic or Bronze Age houses. Shallow depressions often show where huts once stood. Most were built in dry stone walling with a roof of branches covered by turf.

Furniture was usually of wood. But at Skara Brae, in Orkney, a shortage of timber forced the villagers to use stone instead. Inside the hut pictured below you can see a central hearth with beds on either side; against the far wall there's a stone dresser and, to the right of it, a pit for shellfish.

My hut circle was at:..

....Score **80**

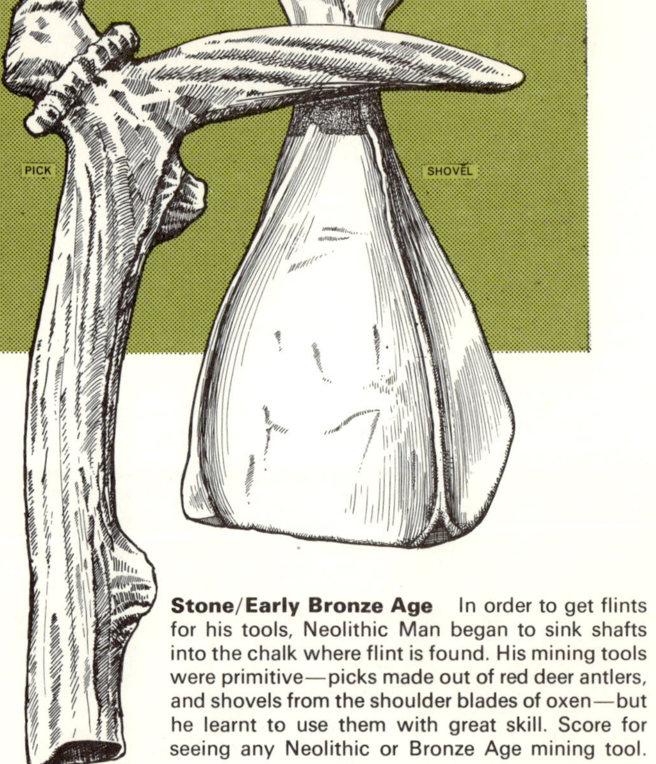

Stone/Early Bronze Age In order to get flints for his tools, Neolithic Man began to sink shafts into the chalk where flint is found. His mining tools were primitive—picks made out of red deer antlers, and shovels from the shoulder blades of oxen—but he learnt to use them with great skill. Score for seeing any Neolithic or Bronze Age mining tool.

Mine was a: ....

At: .... Score **40**

Stone/Early Bronze Age Grime's Graves at Weeting, Norfolk, are probably the best known Neolithic flint mines in Britain. From a distance they are a confused mass of mounds and hollows, but one shaft with galleries is kept open by the Ministry of the Environment. The name, incidentally, comes from the fact that people used to think this curious area might be the Devil's (or Grim's) burial place.

Neolithic Man had to dig down to the valuable floorstone flint about 25 feet below the surface. Score for seeing any Neolithic or Bronze Age flint mine.

Mine was at:..

....

.... Score **90**

GRIMES' GRAVES

Stone/Early Bronze Age Flint was not the only stone used by Neolithic and Bronze Age craftsmen. Axe heads were often made from hard volcanic stone such as basalt. Compare **A, B** and **C** with **D** and **E.**

Note here the place where you've seen something similar to any one of these:

....

.... Score **40**

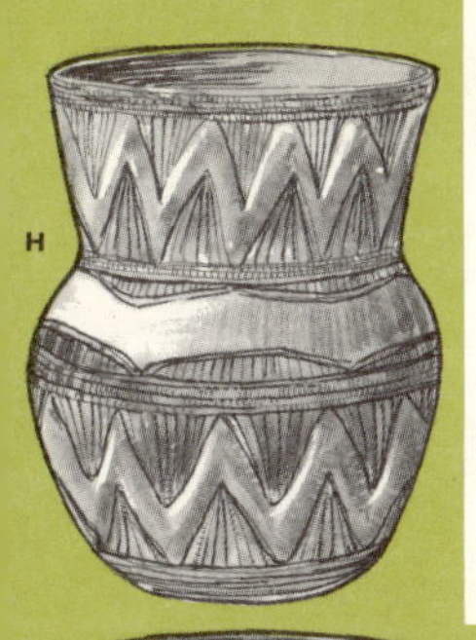

A Flint dagger **B** Flint Scraper **C** Flint leaf-shaped arrowhead **D** Polished axe-head (of volcanic tuff) **E** Polished axe-head with shaft hole of basalt **F** Smooth black Neolithic bowl **G** Later Neolithic bowl of the Peterborough type **H** Early Bronze Age necked beaker **I** Early Bronze Age bell beaker **J** Two Neolithic pottery spoons.

Bronze Age Megalithic tomb A tomb for collective burial—of a class of people, perhaps, or of a family. Between 1500 and 2000 survive in Britain and they can be divided into two main types: gallery graves and passage graves. The first has a burial chamber with a narrow passage leading to the outside of the mound (usually round) that covers it; the second has long stone passages, sometimes divided into sections, beneath a long mound. The one pictured here is Bryn Celli Ddu, a famous passage grave at Anglesey.

When a Megalithic tomb has lost its mound of earth—to reveal blocks of stone supporting a single capstone, it's known as a Cromlech or Dolmen (*right*).

Standing stone (*below*) Found in many moorland regions. Some may be stacks, the results of natural erosion; but others may be the sole survivors of Megalithic tombs, or part of a vanished stone circle or processional way. These are the Devil's Arrows at Boroughbridge, Yorkshire, the tallest of which is 22 feet high.

Long barrows Built by Neolithic farmers as a burial place for the family of a chieftain or other important persons. About 200 survive in Britain. Most are mounds of earth or chalk about 100–300 feet long, 30–100 feet wide and 4–12 feet high. You'll sometimes spot one rising from the middle of a farmer's field, perhaps with a dense growth of trees covering it.

My long barrow was at:..........................

....

....

....

.... Score **70**

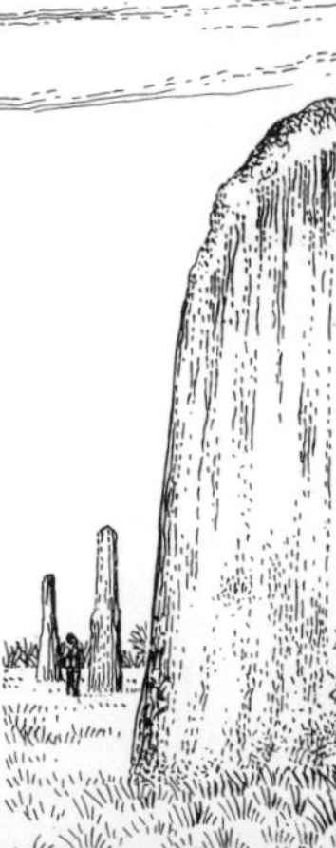

Stone Age Stonehenge The most famous prehistoric temple in Europe. First laid out by Secondary Neolithic people between 1900 and 1700 BC, then altered several times. The great stone circle we know today dates from about 1400 BC.

When you visit Stonehenge yourself, remember to look for the carving of a dagger and axe-heads, which was recently spotted on the sarsen stones—look on the inside face (about four feet from the ground) of the third upright in the sarsen horseshoe—counting clockwise from the open end.

What was the name of the stone circle you visited?

....

....

.... Score **40**

Here's a lintel lying on its side so you can see the mortise holes; and another in position on two uprights (which have projecting knobs or tenons on top). The lintels were probably raised foot by foot on stacked lengths of timber.

The stones used in Stonehenge are sandstone, quarried locally, and blue stone which might have been hauled all the way from the Prescelly Hills in Pembrokeshire, Wales.

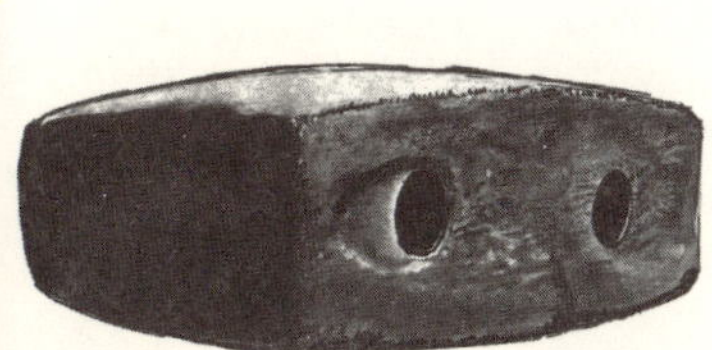

Crop Marks Using aircraft and cameras, archaeologists are now able to discover new sites even when there is nothing apparently visible above the ground. The reason is simple. After a hole or ditch has been dug, it gradually silts up again with soil. Since it absorbs water more easily and has a higher humus content than the land surrounding it, vegetation grows taller on this new soil.

If on the other hand, there is buried stone-work below the surface, vegetation will be shorter than normal—as you can see in the diagram.

You may see patterns in grass and other vegetation, but crops planted by man provide the best background. Barley is said to be the most effective, followed by wheat and oats.

When you look down from an aircraft or the top of a hill, these differences of height are transformed into patterns showing, perhaps, the outline of buildings, trackways, forts or settlements.

See if you can spot crop marks yourself. All you need is good luck and a hill, the steeper the better, which overlooks a field of crops.

The crop marks in this photograph show round barrows *(see page 18)*.

I-SPYed crop marks at:..

....

....Score **100**

Bronze/Iron Age Round Barrows These are our most numerous prehistoric monuments. Despite destruction by farming and other developments, there are still between 10,000 and 20,000 round barrows in Britain. They were a final covering of a sacred area for the dead. They may be 15–100 feet across and 20 or more feet high. The different types are shown below.

Bodies were often buried with tools, weapons and food to help in the next life. The tools and weapons were sometimes broken to release the spirits believed to live in them. Some of these are shown on the page opposite.

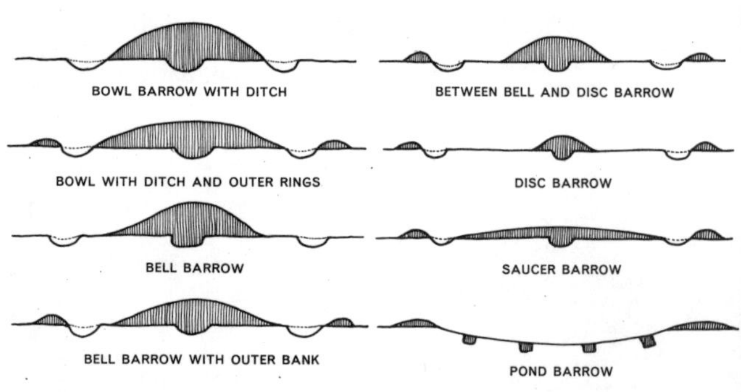

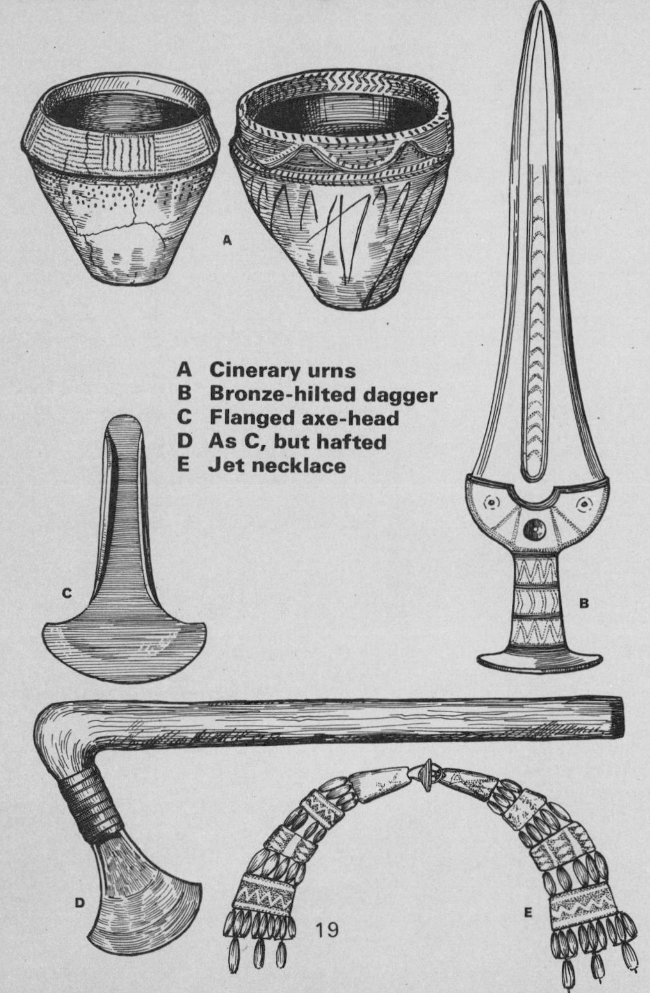

A Cinerary urns
B Bronze-hilted dagger
C Flanged axe-head
D As C, but hafted
E Jet necklace

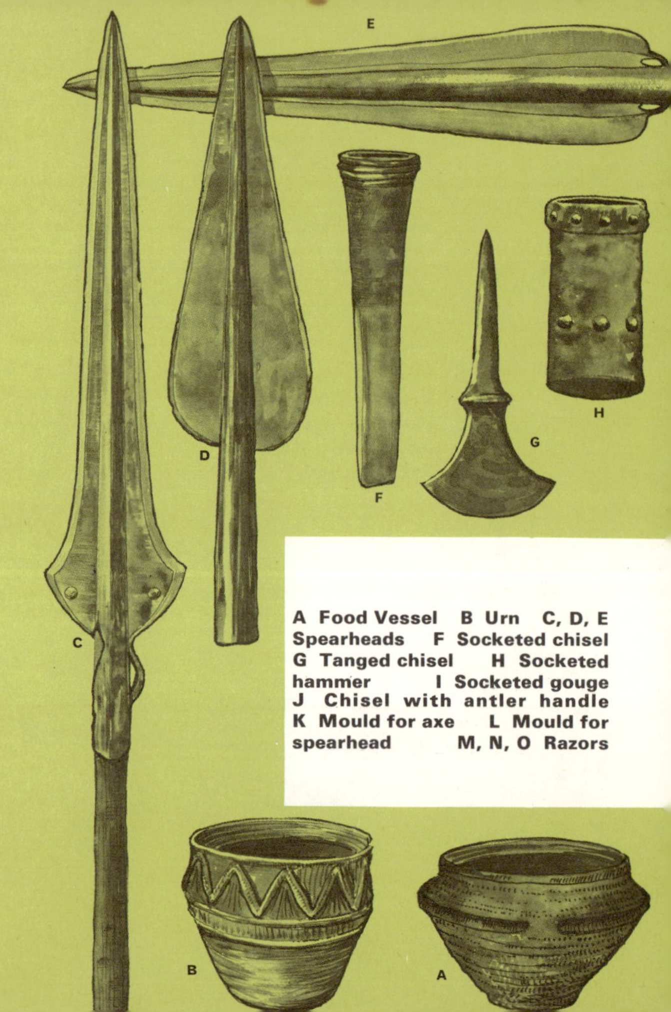

A Food Vessel B Urn C, D, E Spearheads F Socketed chisel G Tanged chisel H Socketed hammer I Socketed gouge J Chisel with antler handle K Mould for axe L Mould for spearhead M, N, O Razors

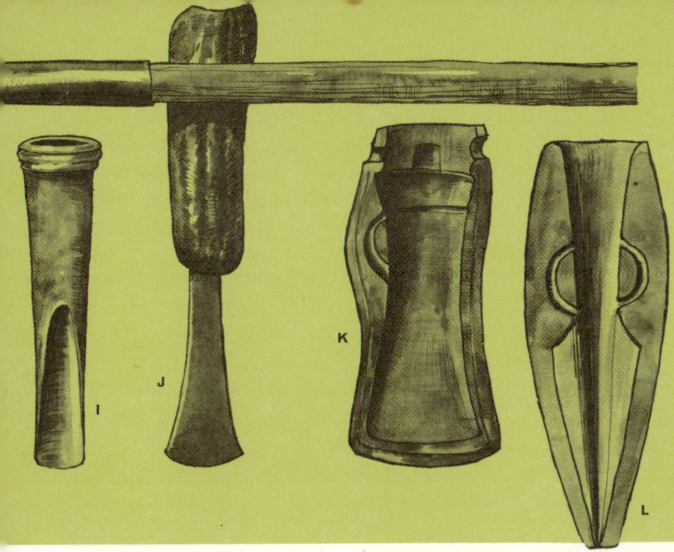

Bronze Age About 1800 BC Britain was invaded by the Beaker people, who brought with them the knowledge of copper. The use of bronze, an alloy of copper and tin, followed gradually.

Name three Bronze Age articles you have seen:............

.... Score **30**

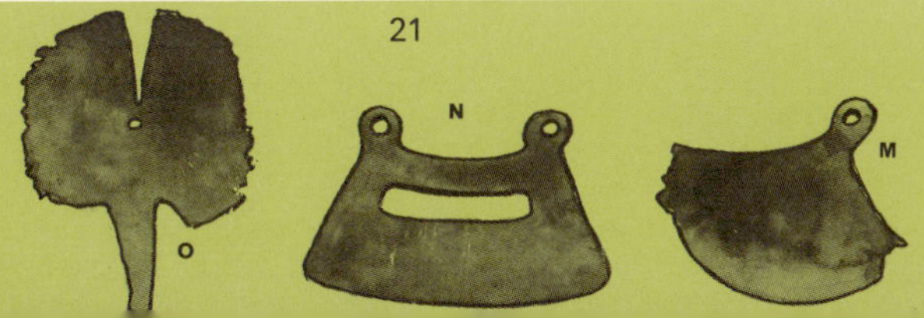

Bronze Age Celtic Fields The plough was first used towards the end of the Bronze Age. It was not heavy enough to be used on any but light soils, and even then cross-ploughing was necessary. The ploughman took the same number of steps in both directions—hence the small square Celtic fields often seen on open downland.

Here is a photograph of the Celtic fields at Smacam Down in Dorset.

Mine were at:...

....

....

....Score **60**

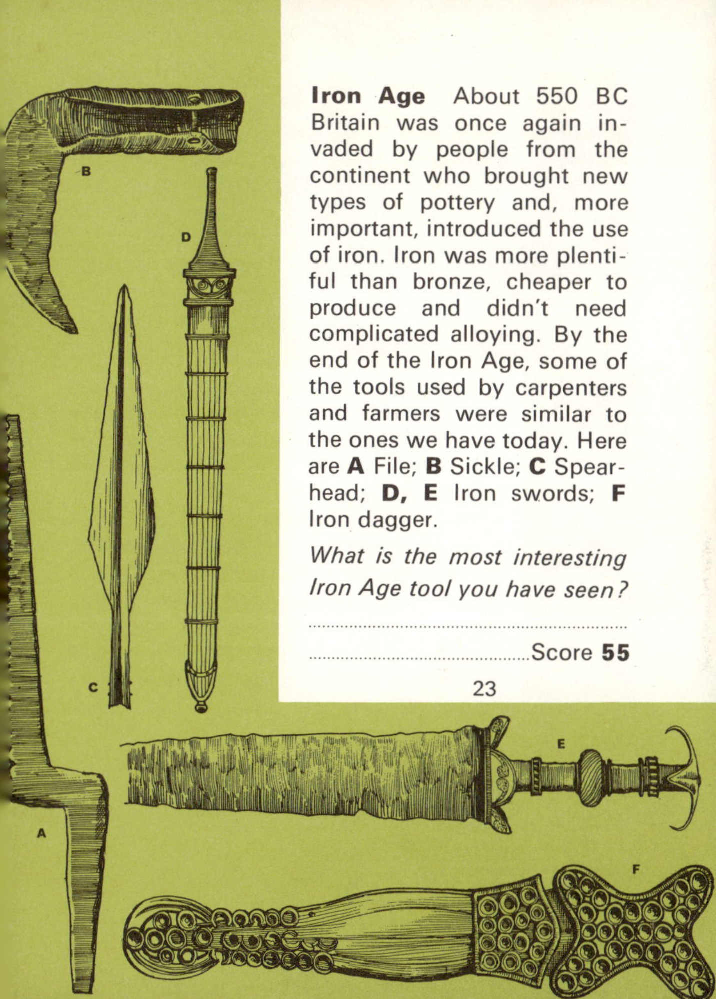

Iron Age About 550 BC Britain was once again invaded by people from the continent who brought new types of pottery and, more important, introduced the use of iron. Iron was more plentiful than bronze, cheaper to produce and didn't need complicated alloying. By the end of the Iron Age, some of the tools used by carpenters and farmers were similar to the ones we have today. Here are **A** File; **B** Sickle; **C** Spearhead; **D, E** Iron swords; **F** Iron dagger.

What is the most interesting Iron Age tool you have seen?

....

....Score **55**

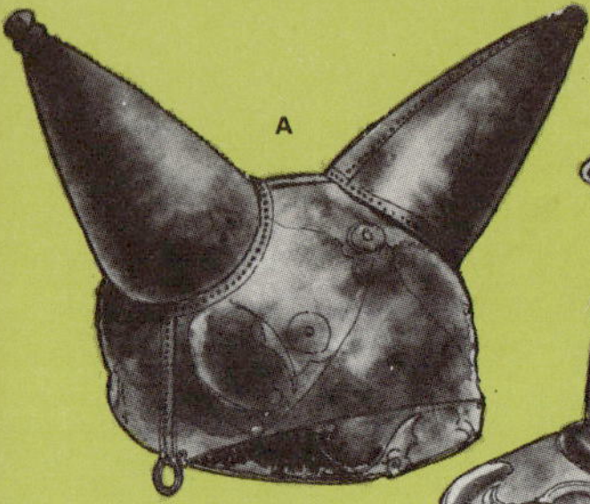

A

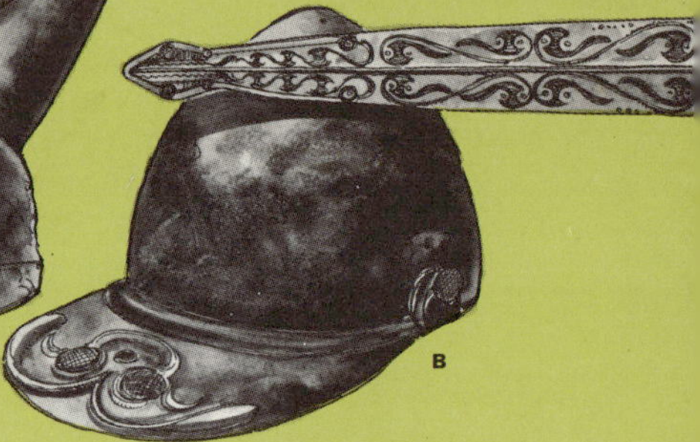

B

C

Iron Age Chieftains of the Iron Age people were sometimes buried with their war chariots. Look in museums for their helmets, shields, horse-harness and chariot fittings.

Here, for example, you see (**A**) A horned helmet from the Thames at Waterloo Bridge (**B**) Helmet with a broad neck guard probably found in northern Britain (**C**) A gold-bronze shield from the Thames at Battersea (**D**) A bronze bridle bit from a chariot-burial at Arras, Yorkshire (**E**) Hollow bronze horn from County Limerick.

NZE SCABBARD WITH CHASED SCROLL-ORNAMENT

Iron Age During the Iron Age B period artistic ideas from the continent became very popular. Craftsmen decorated nearly every smooth metal surface with fine scroll and spiral patterns. Red enamel work was sometimes used to imitate coral studs. This bronze mirror found at Desborough, Northants, is probably the finest specimen of Iron Age art in Britain. It was made early in the first century AD.

What were the Iron Age articles you saw and where did you see them?

....

....

....

....

.... Score **30**

DESBOROUGH MIRROR

Iron Age To protect themselves the earliest Iron Age invaders built hilltop forts—simply an outer ditch and a revetment—a wall of stone or wooden stakes, with earthen ramparts behind. Between the ditch and the revetment was a berm, an exposed ledge where attackers would come under heavy fire.

Here's another form of defence, a Scottish broch, a tall circular tower built as a stronghold by an Iron Age chief who probably combined farming with raiding.

Where was your Iron Age hill fort? ....

....

....

.... Score **50**

MAIDEN CASTLE, DORSET

Iron Age As weapons improved and new ones—such as the sling—were introduced, so the strength of hill forts had to increase. It may, of course, have worked the other way too; new weapons were necessary to overcome stronger defences. Hill forts built during the Iron Age B period had extra ramparts and an entrance designed so attackers couldn't ride or drive straight in.

The famous Maiden Castle in Dorset, shown here, was once a Neolithic causewayed camp; it then became an early Iron Age fort and finally one of the most important forts in Britain. It was stormed and taken by the Roman Second Legion in AD 45.

Iron Age A small group of Iron Age B people settled in Somerset and gave the name 'lake-village' to some of their settlements. This can be rather misleading since the famous villages at Meare and Glastonbury were in fact built on artificial islands in the marshes.

They were not occupied for long—probably established about 50 BC and abandoned soon after Roman power extended across the country. Though hardly important villages of their time they now give an almost unique picture of Iron Age B life. Moisture and a covering of peat have preserved carts, dug-out canoes, baskets, wooden bowls and knives still in their hafts—all things that seldom survive at a hill-village site.

GLASTONBURY LAKE-VILLAGE
(model in Taunton Museum)

Iron Age The people of Glastonbury lake village used the rotary quern for grinding grain, and their pottery can be recognised by its graceful wavy decoration. The potter's wheel was introduced during this period.

On the pottery look for horizontal streak marks left by the potter's fingers. You may also see string marks on the base, showing how the pot was detached from the wheel. Look for both these marks—shown below—on later Iron Age pottery and note down where you saw them.

Finger marks: .... Score **60**

String marks: .... Score **60**

STATER (*LEFT*) AND CELTIC COPIES

Iron Age When the Belgae, or Iron Age C people, began invading Britain about 100 BC, they introduced the idea of coinage. Until then, trade had been based on barter, with flat iron currency bars serving as money (*below*). Their first coins were copied from Gaulish ones; later, coins were copied from the gold stater of Philip of Macedon. The illustration above shows how, in the process of copying, the original design altered until it became completely unrecognisable.

Where did you see your Iron Age currency?....................

....Score **80**

IRON CURRENCY BARS

Iron Age The long lean figure of a horse appears on many Iron Age coins—a Celtic version of a Greek design—and is also to be seen cut into a chalk hill-side at Uffington, Berkshire. Some say it was a standard cut by King Alfred after his victory at Ashdown; others that it represented the dragon slain by St. George. But now we know it was cut in the first or second century BC, probably by the Atrebates tribe who held Uffington castle—in the background.

Not all hill figures date from the Iron Age. Most are medieval or quite recent. Two others that are probably Celtic are the Cerne Abbas Giant, Dorset and the Long Man of Wilmington, Sussex.

Which early hill figure have you seen?..............................

....Score **30**

WHITE HORSE AT UFFINGTON, BERKSHIRE

Roman We travel on many of them today and they link some of our most historic towns. Roman roads are the most lasting impression we have of the Romans. They were built to link forts and towns, to be used all the year round in all weathers.

They usually ran along an agger, or embankment, with a ditch on either side, and they often ran for great distances in a straight line. Look at this air photograph of Foss Way, which ran from Lincoln to Exeter. It shows a modern road built exactly on top of the Roman one.

Score for walking or driving along any Roman road—whether a modern highway, a narrow lane between high hedges, or just a faint ridge across a field.

Mine was at:..

....

....

....

....Score **20**

Roman The next great Roman work remaining in Britain is the magnificent Hadrian's Wall. It was a barrier stretching from the mouth of the Tyne to the Solway Firth, 18 feet high and 9 feet thick, with a vallum, or ditch, on the south side. Along its length of 73 miles a series of mile castles were built at intervals of a Roman mile.

The best place to see remains of the wall is at Housesteads, Northumberland, where you'll also see the ruins of a wall-fort and its attendant village.

Further north was the Antonine Wall, a barrier on turf running from the Forth to the Clyde. It was much weaker than Hadrian's Wall and was abandoned after 54 years.

Which Roman fort have you seen?.......................................

....Score **50**

Roman Immediately after the conquest, Roman merchants began to settle by the lowest crossing place of the Thames. The new town, called Londinium, became an important road junction, sea port and military depot. In AD 61 it was attacked and destroyed by a tribe led by Queen Boudicca, or Boadicea; but it was quickly rebuilt, and eventually the population grew to more than 30,000.

At the end of the first century, when Londinium was still an open city, a rectangular fort was built to the north west, in an area now called Cripplegate. When about 100 years later, a city wall was built it incorporated two sides of the fort into its length. The wall was at least 20 feet high and 9 feet thick. Small sections, like the one below, still remain.

On the page opposite are some Roman fortifications still to be seen in Britain: **A** Newport Arch, Lincoln; **B** Burgh Castle, Great Yarmouth; **C** Multangular Tower, York; **D** Bastion and town wall, Caerwent.

B
REMAINING
ROMAN WALLS
A
D
C

Roman Many of our towns date from the Roman period. Some began as trading settlements outside forts; others, such as Gloucester, were founded for soldiers demobilised from the legions. Lincoln is another colonia of this kind.

Many towns had, outside their walls, amphitheatres for public games, spectacles and gladiator fights.

Public baths were an important part of Roman social life. You met your friends there, exchanged news and gossip, even arranged business deals. After bathing you enjoyed a rub-down with olive oil and a massage with a metal scraper or *strigil*.

On the opposite page: **A** oil can and strigils; **B** nail cleaner with tweezers; **C** Bone comb; **D** Ligula, used for taking cosmetics from the narrow glass phials in which they were kept; **E** Ear-scoop.

Score for seeing any Roman bath or hypocaust—an underfloor heating system shown below.

Mine was at: ....

....Score **70**

HYPOCAUST SYSTEM, CHEDWORTH

ROMAN BATHS, BATH

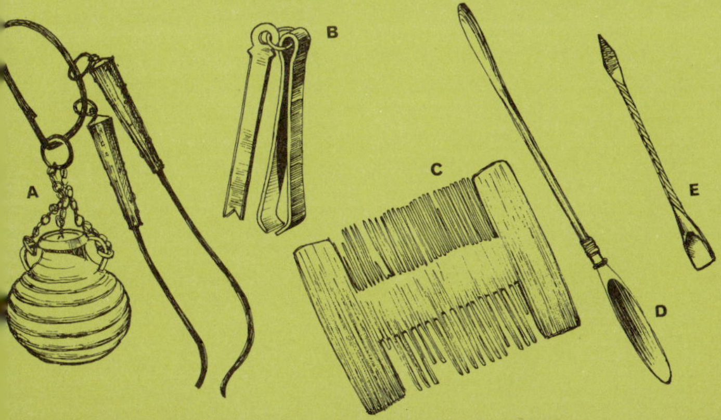

A

B

C

D

E

Roman weight A steelyard was a metal bar, marked in pounds and ounces, with a hook for handling goods to be weighed. You moved the weight along the bar until it balanced.

Amphora Wine was imported from Italy, Spain and Gaul in large pottery amphorae, often 3–4 feet long. You either left them lying on their sides or stood them in a hole in the ground *(bottom left)*.

Religion After prohibiting Druidism the Romans were very tolerant about which gods the Britons worshipped. They even added Celtic gods to their own long list of deities. Here's an altar, one of a group a centurion dedicated to twelve different gods.

Chi-Rho Monogram (*below*) Christianity became the official religion in 312 A.D.; watch for this early Christian monogram on villa floors and on pewter or silver ware.

Roman tools Score for seeing any one of these: **A** saw; **B** combined axe and hammer; **C** carpenter's chisel, about 10 inches long; **D** two bits, for fitting into a brace.

I saw a: ....

....

At: ....

....Score **50**

LULLINGSTONE VILLA

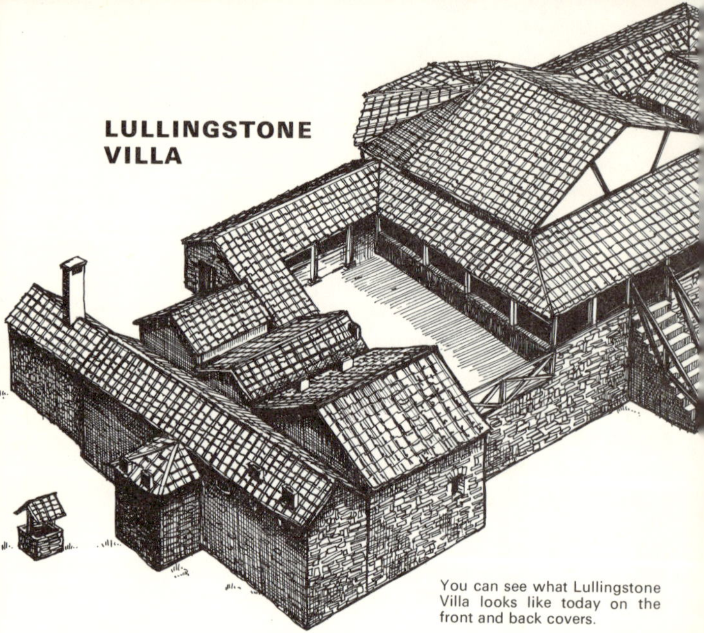

You can see what Lullingstone Villa looks like today on the front and back covers.

Roman Roman farmers often built luxurious houses—or villas—on their estates. Lullingstone Villa in

CUP

BOWL

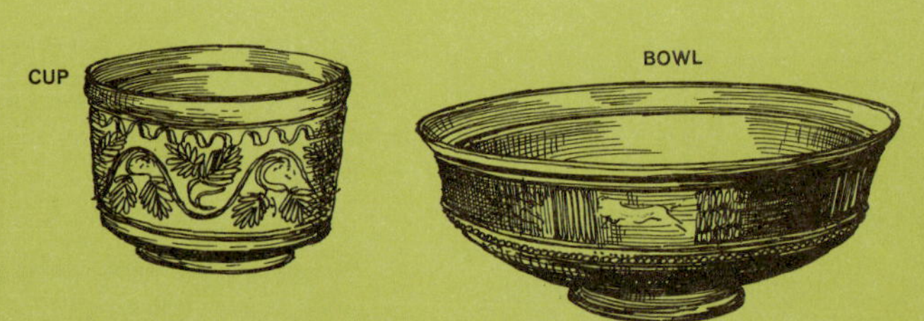

Kent, shown opposite as it must have looked between 33 and 380 A.D., is a typical example. It was built in the first century, rebuilt and replanned several times, and finally destroyed by fire early in the fifth century.

The hard red pottery which the Romans mass produced and sold throughout their empire is called Samian ware. Two examples, a cup and a bowl, are shown opposite.

Glass vessels, like the five below, and window glass, were also  imported in great quantities from Italy, Gaul and the Rhineland. There were glass furnaces in Britain, however, at Castor and Wilderspool.

Where did you see your Roman villa? ....

.... Score **80**

GLASS FLASKS AND BOTTLES
(all bluish green in colour)

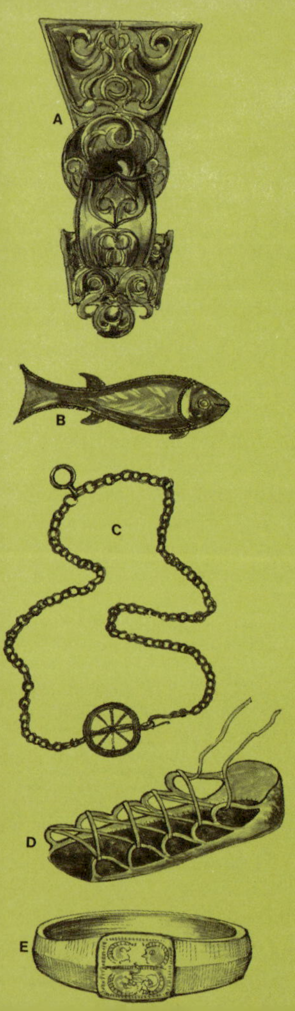

ROMAN ORNAMENTS

A Celtic-style brooch, known as the Aesica Brooch, and decorated in true Celtic manner with embossed spiral scrolls. This is a good example of the way in which native art continued to flourish during the Roman occupation.

B Roman brooch Bronze. Enamelled green and white and used instead of a button.

C Gold chain A personal ornament.

D Sandal A man's sandal, about 11 inches long, which laced up round the lower leg. Boots with studded soles, sandals and scraps of leather are sometimes found in areas where Roman shoemakers had shops—near the Bank of England for instance.

E Finger ring Silver. The square bezel is engraved with four helmeted heads.

What Roman ornament have you seen?..

....Score **50**

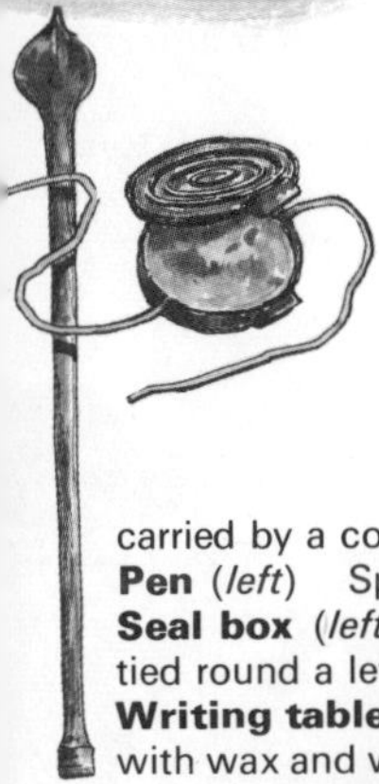

The Romans wrote on wax-surfaced wooden tablets with sharp-pointed metal styli; and on papyrus or parchment with split-nibbed pens rather like the ones we use today. Here's a selection of Roman writing equipment: **Inkwells** (*above*) The one on the left is of red clay; the smaller one is bronze, with a lid, and could be carried by a cord tied to metal loops at the sides.

Pen (*left*) Split-nibbed pen of bronze.

Seal box (*left*) This protected the wax seal on string tied round a letter or document.

Writing tablet (*below*) Made of wood. You spread it with wax and wrote with a pointed stylus.

The Romans were forbidden to bury their dead within town limits, so cemeteries and tombs are usually found along the roads leading from towns and forts.

Cinerary urn After cremation, ashes were buried in stone, pottery or glass urns. The lead canister contained a glass cinerary urn.

Tomb Usually dedicated to the gods of the under-world. Look for the words Dis Manibus, sometimes abbreviated to D.M. Here's the reconstructed tomb of Julius Classicianus, procurator (or civil governor) of Britain.

CANISTER

CINERARY URN

Protecting our past Stonehenge and other famous sites are in the care of the Department of the Environment; so, too, are hundreds of smaller sites such as barrows and burial mounds. These signs help protect them:

Star sign (A) For areas used by the Army or other Services. It warns tank drivers, for instance, not to drive over a long barrow. Made of aluminium and not painted.

Scheduling notice plate (B) Warns that no-one may damage or develop the site.

Guardianship notice plate (C) Indicates monument open to the public.

Not everyone knows the meaning of these signs. So if you see someone bulldozing a burial mound or filling in the ditch of a camp marked with one of these signs, tell your local archaeological society immediately.

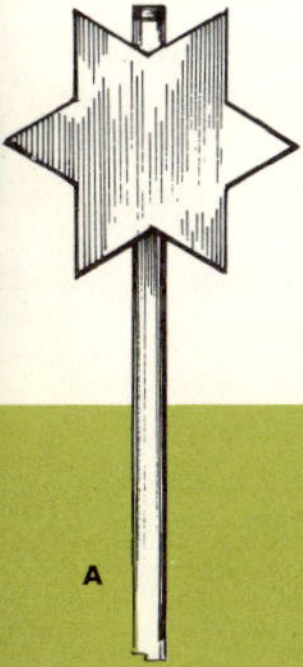

A

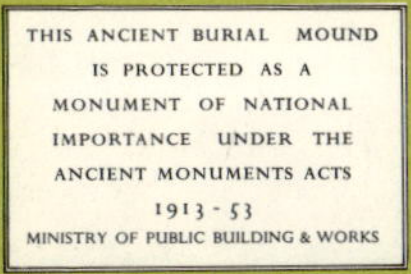

B

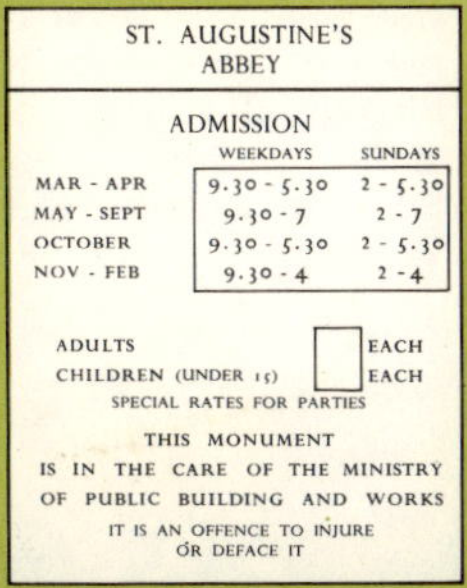

THIS ANCIENT BURIAL MOUND
IS PROTECTED AS A
MONUMENT OF NATIONAL
IMPORTANCE UNDER THE
ANCIENT MONUMENTS ACTS
1913 - 53
MINISTRY OF PUBLIC BUILDING & WORKS

C

ST. AUGUSTINE'S
ABBEY

ADMISSION

	WEEKDAYS	SUNDAYS
MAR - APR	9.30 - 5.30	2 - 5.30
MAY - SEPT	9.30 - 7	2 - 7
OCTOBER	9.30 - 5.30	2 - 5.30
NOV - FEB	9.30 - 4	2 - 4

ADULTS EACH
CHILDREN (UNDER 15) EACH
SPECIAL RATES FOR PARTIES

THIS MONUMENT
IS IN THE CARE OF THE MINISTRY
OF PUBLIC BUILDING AND WORKS
IT IS AN OFFENCE TO INJURE
OR DEFACE IT

ELECTRUM TORQUE (SNETTISHAM TREASURE)

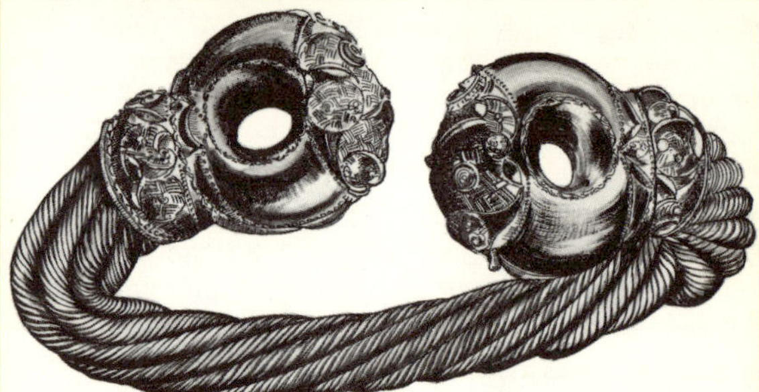

Treasure Trove When threatened by war or other danger, people sometimes buried their precious possessions for safety. And, in some cases, they've remained buried until the present day.

In November 1950, for instance, a fabulous hoard was ploughed up near Snettisham, Norfolk. Christened the 'Snettisham Treasure', it included three electrum torques and a hollow gold bracelet, delicately ornamented. A torque was worn around the neck.

Finds like this are called Treasure Trove and are, by law, the property of the Crown. However, the finder, not the owner of the land, is either given back the find, or its full market value. If you should find anything of value, gold or silver objects in particular, you should tell the Coroner for the district (you can reach him through the local police) or write to the Director, British Museum, London, WC1B 3DG.

Score for seeing any Treasure Trove in a museum.

Mine was a: ....

At: .... Score **55**

JOIN THE I-SPY TRIBE

- All you need to become a full member of the I-SPY Tribe is an I-SPY Membership Pack which includes an I-SPY badge and secret code book. Buy one from your newsagent or bookshop today!
- Wear your I-SPY badge everywhere. You'll find it an *Open Sesame* to all kinds of places.
- Tell your friends about I-SPY. Invite them to join and form a Patrol with you.
- Collect all the I-SPY books—and you'll have a wonderful library of your own.
- Write to me about any interesting discoveries you make. You may win a prize!

**Big Chief I-SPY, Wigwam-by-the-Green,
382-386 Edgware Road, London W2 1EP**

I-SPY BOOKS

AT THE SEASIDE
FARM ANIMALS
HISTORY
IN THE COUNTRY
IN THE STREET
ON THE ROAD
LONDON FROM TRAFALGAR SQUARE
CHURCHES
WILD FLOWERS
BUTTERFLIES AND MOTHS
TREES
PETS
THE SKY
BIRDS
HORSES AND PONIES
ON A CAR JOURNEY
ON A TRAIN JOURNEY
DOGS
FISHING
CARS
STAMPS
CAR NUMBERS
BUSES AND COACHES
CIVIL AIRCRAFT
IN THE WOOD
BRITISH COINS
FOOTBALL
CRICKET
AT THE AIRPORT
SHIPS AND BOATS
ANIMALS AT THE ZOO
BIRDS AND REPTILES AT THE ZOO
BRITISH WILDLIFE
ON THE MOTORWAY
CATS
IN THE HEDGEROW
LORRIES AND VANS

INDEX

Acheulian Hand-axe 4
Aesica Brooch 42
Amphora 38
Antonine Wall 33
Arrowheads 6, 10
Awl, antler/bone 5
Axe 4, 10, 18, 39
Barrow:
Long 13
Round 17, 18
Bath, Roman 36
Beaker, Bronze Age 11
Beaker People 21
Belgae 30
Boudicca (or Boadicea) .. 34
Broch, Scottish 26
Bryn Celli Ddu 12
Burgh Castle 34
Celtic fields 22
Chi-Rho Monogram 39
Chisel 20, 39
Cinerary Urn:
Bronze Age 18
Roman 44
Clactonian flake-tool 4
Classicianus, Julius 44
Coin, Celtic 30
Colonia 36
Copper 21
Cromlech 12
Crop-marks 16
Currency bar 30
Desborough Mirror 25
Devil's Arrows 13
Dolmen 12
Flint mines 8
Fort:
Hillfort 26
Roman 34
Foss Way 32
Gallery Grave 12
Glass, Roman 42
Glastonbury 28–29
Grime's Graves 9
Grimscote furrows 22
Guardianship notice plate .. 45
Hadrian's Wall 33
Hammer 5, 20, 39
Harpoon, antler 6
Helmet, Bronze Age 24
Hill figure 31
Housesteads, Roman fort .. 33
Hut circle 7
Hypocaust 36
Iron 23
Lake-village 28
Leister 6
Ligula 36
Lincoln 32, 34, 36
Londinium 34
London Wall 34
Long Man, Wilmington .. 31
Lullingstone Roman Villa .. 41
Maiden Castle 27
Megalithic tomb 12
Microlith 6
Necklace, Bronze Age .. 18
Passage grave 12
Pick, antler 5
Potter's wheel 29
Quern, rotary 29
Roman Britain 32
Samian Ware 41
Scheduling notice plate .. 45
Seal-box, Roman 43
Shield, Iron Age 24
Shovel, antler 8
Sickle, Iron Age 23
Smacam Down 22
Skara Brae hut 7
Snettisham Treasure 46
Standing stone 13
Star sign 45
Steelyard Weight 38
Stonehenge 14–15
Strigil 36
Swanscombe Man 4
Sword, Iron Age 23
Tomb:
Megalithic 12
Roman 44
Torque 46
Treasure Trove 46
Uffington, white horse .. 31
Villa, Roman 41
York 34

Printed by Loxley Brothers Limited of Sheffield and published for the proprietors by Polystyle Publications Ltd., 382/386 Edgware Road, London W2 1EP

I SBN 85096760 0